LITTLE BOOK OF
TRACTION ENGINES

Steve Lanham

LITTLE BOOK OF
TRACTION ENGINES

First published in the UK in 2012

© G2 Entertainment Limited 2012

www.G2ent.co.uk

Printed and bound printed in the China

ISBN 978-1-907803-35-2

Contents

Introduction

ABOVE
1904 Fowler
No.9904 towing
a barge load
during the 1930s.
This locomotive
is now preserved
in Sweden.
*(National Motor
Museum/MPL)*

For more than a hundred years the traction engine was a familiar sight, working the fields or roving the highways and byways of Britain, Europe and beyond. First proposed as a replacement for the horse-drawn plough, it revolutionised agricultural processes, easing the tasks of cultivation, tillage, reaping, threshing and baling. In the woodyard, the saw bench was introduced and this cost effective way of mechanising timber production was further enhanced by an ability to move heavier loads and employ fewer labourers.

The traction engine's immense practicalities were, in time, realised by fair and circus operators nationwide, and businesses great and small seized on the advantages of transporting bulk goods and household commodities using steam power. The humble roller greatly improved road surfacing for the benefit of all traffic including the heavy haulage locomotive that could shift colossal objects too large to move by rail or canal. As the 20th Century dawned, new legislation allowed lighter vehicles to be operated singlehandedly and for a comparatively short time, steam tractors and wagons formed a considerable portion of vehicle manufacture.

As internal combustion engined vehicles became more reliable and the number of motor manufacturers increased, locomotive owners embraced the new technology switching to petrol and diesel lorries and tractors, irrevocably sealing the fate of the working steam-driven vehicle. Fortunately, there were many forward-thinking enthusiasts who anticipated the demise and set about rescuing and restoring these wonderful machines for us, the future generations, to enjoy.

One of my earliest childhood recollections is from July 1974. In pouring rain, Mum had taken us out for a drive in our Volkswagen Variant to see 1912 Aveling & Porter roller No.7807 *Jersey Lily* on her journey to the Isle of Wight steam rally. My Dad was helping

ABOVE
1915 Foster showman's tractors No.14066, *Endeavour* and No.14205, *Obsession*.

owner John Young move the roller on the first leg to the Sealink ferry terminal at Lymington and when we found them they were taking on water at Brockenhurst. For the last few miles my brother, Keith, who is four years older than me was offered a ride on the footplate. I, on the other hand, was too young and after all it was raining! If memory serves me right, *Jersey Lily* was

ABOVE A locomotive regularly driven with the help of the author's father to rallies during the 1960s and 70s was 1913 Wallis & Steevens Expansion engine No. 7293, *Pandora*, seen here at an overnight stop on Salisbury Plain in 1972.

laden with living van and Land Rover and as I watched, green with three-year-old envy, she rumbled up the road, Dad waving cheerfully and Keith hanging on for dear life! As smoke curled off into the distance, Mum put the Variant into gear and off home we drove again with me sat in the back, clenching and unclenching my little fists, seething that I wasn't part of the adventure! It was probably not long after this that Dad decided to concentrate his weekends and days off with his young family and pretty much called time on driving traction engines.

It wasn't until years later and a chance meeting with Mike Doherty that I was finally able to fulfil that childhood ambition. Mike was carrying out some maintenance work at Milestones Museum, Basingstoke on the day I happened to be installing a travelling exhibition, and during a break we started chatting. For more than twenty years, Mike has been the proud owner of *Monarch*, a 10-ton Babcock & Wilcox road roller built in 1926, and when he realised my enthusiasm, kindly offered the chance for me to help out the next time she was in steam. A few

weeks later, on a bright crisp morning, I found myself watching *Monarch* gently simmering, raising steam ahead of what would turn out to be a thoroughly enjoyable morning trundling along a dozen or so miles of sun-dappled New Forest lanes between Ower, Lyndhurst

and Burley. Since then, Mike has asked me to assist him and his band of regular helpers on numerous occasions including the 23-mile journey from Burley to Tarrant Hinton - showground for the world-famous Great Dorset Steam Fair. Today, most owners choose

to low-load their locomotives to rallies and events, so I feel especially privileged to be able to join a great team of people on the increasingly rare occasion a vehicle such as this is seen working on the road.

When I was asked to write *The Little Book of Traction Engines*, I quite literally jumped at the chance – what better way to spend your work time than to

casting out the smell of coal smoke, steam and oil that is such a defining memory of my childhood – I guess there's steam in the blood!

In putting this book together, I would like to thank the following people for their help and unstinting support: Patrick Collins of the Reference Library and Jon Day of the Motoring Picture Library at the National Motor Museum, Beaulieu; Wendy Bowen of Hampshire Museums Service; Mike Dyson of the National Traction Engine Trust; Nigel Spender for access to the restoration archive of his Aveling & Porter road roller No.12335; and Michael Bennett, Peter Brownrigg, Richard Maddox, Abbie Stone and my Dad, Mike Lanham, for providing the many colour images featured in these pages. Finally, I would like to express my wholehearted appreciation to Mike, Les, Bob, Nigel, Fred and of course *Monarch* for the opportunity to indulge many happy hours steaming through the Hampshire and Dorset countryside, and always in great company.

Steve Lanham, 2010

research, write and reminisce about that wonderful thing, the traction engine. There is nothing quite like the sight and sound of one of these magnificent machines pounding along the highway,

A History Of The Traction Engine: In The Beginning...

The fundamental energy producing characteristics of steam were realised as far back as pre-Christian times and it is recorded that in the 1st Century AD Greek mathematician, Heron of Alexandria, made several toy vehicles that were self-propelled by steam. But the idea was never significantly progressed as a source of stationary or motive power until the 17th Century.

In the first quarter of the 1600s, David Ramsey and Thomas Wildgoose announced a machine that could plough fields without the aid of horses. Ramsey developed the idea, suggesting steam as the source of power, but there seems to be no evidence to prove that Ramsey's Patent of 1630 was ever put into practice.

In 1672, astronomer, scientist and Flemish Jesuit missionary, Father Ferdinand Verbiest, is said to have designed a steam trolley for the Emperor Kangxi of China. Similar to Heron's efforts, it was presented as a toy for the Emperor's amusement and featured a spherical boiler emitting a thin jet of steam on to a simple turbine that, through primitive gearing, drove the rear wheels. The trolley was not large or strong enough to accommodate a person and there appear to be no records of a full-size version ever being made.

Many inventors experimented with the concept of steam power, but it was

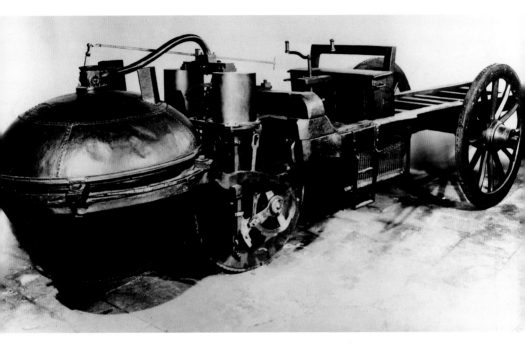

not until 1712 that a steam-driven engine was first put to practical use. Thomas Newcomen's atmospheric beam engine, constructed at the Dudley Castle mine, Tipton, worked on the principle that when steam condensed within a cylinder, it formed a partial vacuum. Cold water was injected into the cylinder to assist the condensing process and suction caused by the vacuum combined with atmospheric pressure would draw a piston down into the cylinder. The piston was connected via a rod to one end of a pivoting beam. On the other end of the beam was another connecting rod with a bucket

ABOVE
1769 Fardier à Vapeur built by Nicolas-Joseph Cugnot. *(National Motor Museum/ MPL)*

attached that, when in motion, lifted flood water from the underground mine. News of the design quickly spread and similar engines were soon to be found assembled and operating in all parts of Europe and beyond.

In 1763, whilst working as a mathematical instrument maker for Glasgow University, James Watt was given the task of repairing a scale model of Newcomen's atmospheric engine. From studying the design, he realised that much of its efficiency was lost when condensing water sprayed into the steam chamber caused the cylinder to rapidly cool down. By introducing a separate condensing chamber, the cylinder could be kept at a more constant temperature. He also sealed the top of the cylinder that on Newcomen's engine had been open to atmospheric pressure and instead forced steam in above the piston. By alternating the injection of steam above and below the piston the engine could perform at greater efficiency and, more importantly, at greater velocity.

Throughout the 1760s, French inventor, Nicolas-Joseph Cugnot, attempted to create a reliable self-propelled vehicle for military use. It was intended that his Fardier à Vapeur would be able to transport some of the heaviest artillery equipment in a time when Louis XV's France was still reeling from the loss of her colonies to Britain during the Seven Years War. By 1769, initial testing had taken place within the Arsenal at Versailles prompting the enthusiastic Lieutenant General Gribeauval and French Foreign Minister the Duke of Choiseul to promote Cugnot's invention to the Marquis de Monteynard, Secretary of State for War. Orders taken for any further vehicles are very unlikely as it proved to be a slow and rather cumbersome beast. During the trials it was required to stop every ten or so minutes in order to build up enough steam pressure again to continue. Another major drawback was its instability, constructed as a three-wheeler with the large steam boiler located ahead of a single and steerable front wheel. This was aptly demonstrated on one particular journey when the vehicle went out of control, careering through a garden wall and overturning – an unfortunate incident that landed Cugnot in the clink!

On Louis XV's death in 1774, he

LEFT
A replica of Richard Trevithick's ungainly steam carriage at the 1996 Victorian Extravaganza, Beaulieu.

IN THE BEGINNING...

was succeeded by his grandson, Louis-Auguste, who was crowned Louis XVI. Largely due to Louis XVI's ill-conceived decisions during his reign, the country was thrown into turmoil, ultimately resulting in the French Revolution. With all the destruction and unrest following the uprising, Cugnot's Fardier à Vapeur was a surprising survivor and in 1800 was presented to the Conservatoire National des Arts et Métiers, Paris. Having latterly endured the ravages of two World Wars, it is still proudly displayed there today, and is generally regarded as the world's first self-propelled vehicle.

During the 1780s, Scotsman Andrew Meikle endeavoured to perfect the threshing drum in an attempt to replace the back-breaking method of hand-held flail threshing (separating grain from husks and straw). According to surveys of the time, 1798 saw the first farm in Britain utilise steam to power its threshing drum. The farm was owned by John Wilkinson, a factory proprietor from Wrexham who also happened to be a business associate of James Watt. Wilkinson's factory was engaged in accurately machining

cylinders for military use such as gun and cannon barrels, but became involved with improving efficiency of the Watt rotary-motion steam engine being built at the time in Birmingham. Wilkinson purchased a number of Watt's engines to mechanise his factory and it is likely that one of these was later transferred to his farm.

By the early 19th Century many industries relied on steam power for economic operation but the engines were slow, large and extremely heavy.

Cornishman, Richard Trevithick, demonstrated the possibilities of a carriage powered by a high pressure steam engine. He had developed the system whilst working as Engineer for the Ding Dong Mine at Penzance where, after a number of Trevithick's modifications, the mine's stationary engine could raise ore and waste products quite efficiently. On Christmas Eve 1801, his cousin, Andrew Vivian, drove the new carriage up Camborne Hill, a steep incline that had previously proved problematic to horse-drawn traffic. A subsequent and more refined Trevithick vehicle called *The London Steam Carriage* was capable of carrying

IN THE BEGINNING...

ten persons and, although it worked well, proved more expensive to operate than a horse carriage. It was marketed and offered for sale but the experiment was eventually abandoned in 1803.

A year later, Trevithick was embroiled in an argument between the owners of two rival South Wales ironworks. One had wagered 500 guineas that Trevithick could build a locomotive capable of pulling a 10-ton load along the ten-mile tramway between Penydarren and Abercynon. He succeeded in winning the bet as the resulting locomotive completed the trip in just over four hours. Its weight, however, almost destroyed the tramway and transportation of pig iron at Penydarren quickly reverted back to pony-haulage. But the age of the railway locomotive had begun.

Over the next twenty years, several attempts were made to perfect the high pressure steam engine with attention drawn to the tricky task of improving the power-to-weight ratio essential for a successful road-going vehicle. But development of anything more sophisticated than horse-drawn agricultural engines, known as

'portables', was partly the consequence of a labour force reluctant to accept modern mechanised technology and partly due to Britain's involvement with the Napoleonic Wars raging in Europe between 1799 and 1815.

During the first quarter of the 19th Century rail travel advanced rapidly from the first fare-paying passengers carried on the Oystermouth Railway in 1807, to the opening of the Stockton & Darlington Railway in 1825, with the likes of George Stephenson's revered locomotive, *Locomotion*, providing motive power.

Rivalry also grew between Goldsworthy Gurney and Walter Hancock, two entrepreneurial inventors.

Having spent much of his youth in Cornwall, Goldsworthy Gurney had, on a visit to Camborne on Christmas Eve 1801, witnessed the demonstration of Richard Trevithick's road-going steam carriage. It must have made quite an impression and stirred the imagination of the young Gurney, as he would later become an accomplished scientist and engineer. Amongst many of his inventions that included the oxy-hydrogen blowpipe,

the steam jet and the Bude-Light (a
dramatic improvement on the hitherto
theatre limelight), he took out a patent
in 1825 for a steam-propelled vehicle
as a possible successor to the horse-
drawn carriage. Two years later his ideas
had evolved into a passenger-carrying
vehicle that outwardly resembled a
stage coach minus the horses. A boiler
was cradled within the framework
at the rear, providing steam for twin
horizontal cylinders located beneath the
carriage body that, through connecting
rods, drove the rear axle. A separate and

smaller dual-acting cylinder provided
lubrication to the motion as well as
forcing air into the furnace at high
velocity, thus maintaining the required
temperature within the boiler. A two-
wheel fore-carriage was added to the
front allowing a coachman to steer the
whole ensemble.

Meanwhile Walter Hancock,
originally of Marlborough, Wiltshire
was, from 1824 to 1836, experimenting
with various forms of steam road
vehicles at his engineering premises in
Stratford, Essex. The most successful

of these, *The Enterprise*, was a purpose-built omnibus that The London & Paddington Steam Carriage Company employed for the first scheduled road-going passenger service to utilise steam power, operating from London Wall via Islington to Paddington. *The Enterprise* incorporated interesting and innovative features that would become common on many later vehicles – a body suspended on leaf springs, the rear axle secured in a swinging arm, and Hancock's own patent artillery wheels. The underslung engine was concealed within the bodywork and powered the rear wheels by a chain working off a crankshaft. Steering was surprisingly well ahead of its time with the direction of the front axle turned through chain link by a steering wheel.

A dispute arose between Hancock and The London & Paddington Steam Carriage Company who ceased operating his vehicle. Nevertheless Hancock continued the service and introduced other versions of the steam carriage.

Gurney's efforts were less successful. The practical capabilities of his steam carriages could not be questioned when one made a journey from London to Bath and back in July 1829, averaging a respectable 14mph but it was, however, not without incident. According to a letter written by his daughter and published in a December 1875 edition of *The Times* newspaper, the machine was set upon by the fearful people of Melksham who threw stones and injured the stoker. Many saw this type of mechanisation as a threat to the labour force and the public seemed even less inclined to ride in proximity to such a dangerous looking boiler. Gurney tried to allay public fears by constructing an articulated vehicle where the engine was positioned away from the passenger car, but to no avail. It is thought two examples of this type were built and indeed the remains of one still survive in the Glasgow Museum of Transport, albeit minus its wheels, boiler and bodywork.

Two months after Gurney's return trip to Bath, the Rainhill Trials were held – a competition to determine the type of locomotive that would be used on the Liverpool & Manchester Railway due to be opened the following year. The trials were a triumph for

RIGHT
A replica
of Robert
Stephenson's
locomotive,
Rocket, here
demonstrated
on the Keighley
& Worth Valley
Railway in 1994.

Robert Stephenson whose celebrated locomotive, *Rocket*, reached a magnificent speed of 29mph. Although *Rocket* was quickly superseded by another of Stephenson's designs, *Planet*, the Liverpool & Manchester Railway transported 460,000 passengers between the two great cities during the first year of service, 1830. The railway's swift, smooth and efficient qualities had quickly gained popularity over the slow, rutted and dusty unpaved roads of the day. It is little wonder, therefore, that steam-operated rail travel won greater public approval than road-going steam carriages such as those of Gurney and Hancock. The damage inflicted by these vehicles to already unsatisfactory road surfaces fuelled opposition and saw hefty charges levied by Turnpike Trusts – private organisations first set up by way of a 1663 Act of Parliament in order to provide a better standard of maintenance to highways.

Not all engines for the home market were so affected by such imposition, however, and engineering manufacturers were able to focus their attention largely on improvements to the non-self propelled portable type instead.

The Halcyon Days Of Steam

The accolade for building the world's first self-moving traction engine should almost certainly go to the Ipswich firm of J. R. & A. Ransome.

The Ransome foundry dated back to the late 18th Century making quality ploughs and agricultural equipment, but at the Royal Liverpool Show in 1841 they had exhibited a vertical boiler portable fitted with a 5hp Birmingham Patent Disc Engine. It also featured a dismountable threshing drum that could be anchored to the ground and driven by a belt connected to the engine's flywheel. In 1842, this quite primitive contraption was displayed at the Bristol Show with a chain-driven rear axle. Although it was capable of 4 or 5mph, it retained an archaic steering system employing a horse to direct the front axle. Several

years later, Ransomes and May, as the firm had then become, unveiled a vehicle described as the 'Farmer's Engine' that bore much resemblance to the later standard traction engine layout. The method of horse-operated steering was replaced by a geared system worked by a steersman standing on a footplate behind the firebox, whilst final drive was via gearing to the rear wheels. The chimney vented from the top of the smokebox at the front of the vehicle although its two cylinders were mounted directly beneath.

As the railway network spread further across the country, road making techniques significantly fell behind. It is not so surprising, therefore, that many names later to become famous engineering firms such as Garrett, Tasker and Aveling & Porter established themselves in rural locations where their

customer base was drawn largely from the surrounding agricultural community.

The 1850s saw much activity in the development of the traction engine during a time of great interest in all things mechanical. For economic reasons, some portable engines were converted to be self-propelled and in 1858 the Royal Agricultural Society ran a competition in Chester for anyone who could introduce a system to replace the horse plough. John Fowler of Leeds had two years previously publicised his use of a solitary portable engine pulling a balance plough across a field by way of windlass, cables and pulleys and it was this technique that won his firm the £500 prize. This enabled Fowler to hone his ideas and later unveil the first ploughing engine incorporating a gear-driven winding drum.

Between 1856 and 1857, William Bray, a ship's engineer from Folkestone, constructed his first road locomotive. Intended for agricultural use, it was designed with Bray's Patent driving wheels featuring teeth that could be made to protrude from the surface of the wheel via an eccentric on the axle, in order to give better grip to the

LEFT
Fowler ploughing engine with gear-driven winding drum, c.1864. *(National Motor Museum/MPL)*

THE HALCYON DAYS OF STEAM

road. In 1859, it was used by circus proprietor, Jim Myers, to haul loaded packing vans between towns so could, in that respect, be regarded as the first showman's engine. With a ship's type steering wheel positioned at the front, the locomotive was driven via twin high pressure outside cylinders through geared shafts to separate final drives on each rear wheel. A clutch system allowed one or the other wheel to be disengaged assisting manoeuvrability when attempting sharp corners – similar to the system employed on today's track laying vehicles such as tanks and bulldozers. The boiler lay in parallel plate frames more akin to a railway locomotive – a practice not uncommon at a time when manufacture was still largely relying on experimentation.

In 1856, a road locomotive equipped with Boydell driving wheels emerged from the Charles Burrell & Sons works in Thetford and was one of the first successful track laying vehicles. The 7-foot wheels featured individual shoes that when in motion locked together forming a flat surface for the wheels to grip – this will be described further in a later chapter.

The Locomotive Acts of 1861 and 1865 imposed a number of conditions that hindered the use of heavy steam engines on Britain's public highways. Clauses detailed under the new legislation stipulated that any vehicle propelled by anything other than animal power should be constructed to consume its own smoke, the penalty for not complying being £5 for each day of vehicle use. Weight was limited to 12 tons and the 10mph speed limit of 1861 was reduced in 1865 to 4mph for the countryside and 2mph for towns. This was further compounded by the provision of a man carrying a red flag walking 60 yards in front to give warning to horse riders and horse-drawn traffic of the approaching vehicle. Not surprisingly, Charles Burrell looked to the overseas market and was able to make improvements to his designs for the benefit of customers mainly in India and South America.

For the 1860s, it was Thomas Aveling of Rochester, Kent, who strove to make the most significant changes and is credited with fine tuning the positioning of locomotive components to what would eventually be regarded

as the standard traction engine layout. Damaging condensation within cylinders had always been a headache for manufacturers and owners alike, but this was rectified in 1861 when Aveling introduced a steam jacket surrounding, and thus preheating, the cylinder block.

He also mounted it on top of the boiler immediately behind the chimney, connected via a short exhaust pipe.

With the crankshaft positioned directly onto the firebox or boiler barrel, vibrations suffered from the state of the highway combined with the

unavoidable stresses from motionwork inevitably caused steam leaks to occur. Once again, Thomas Aveling came up with the solution, altering the plates that formed the sides of the firebox. By extending these 'hornplates' upwards, they could support the crankshaft and gearing away from the locomotive's main 'body' components thus reducing vibration – another idea quickly adopted by virtually all other manufacturers.

General opinion including those championing the expansion of the rail network continued to criticise the weight of road locomotives as being detrimental to the country's highways, but it was Aveling who instead recognised the road *improvement* capabilities of the traction engine. By sheer weight alone, loose stones and gravel were flattened into the road's surface. His 1865 traction engine design, incorporating smooth 3-foot wide wheels of 7-foot diameter and towing a rolling drum made independently by Easton, Amos & Anderson of Erith, were Aveling & Porter's first foray into the production of road rollers that would, over the subsequent seventy or so years, see the company become the world leaders in this field.

The introduction of high strength

Up until the late 18th Century, most engines had been built with single cylinders. They actually worked well but around 1780, Jonathan Hornblower noticed that half of steam pressure taken from the boiler to force the piston through the cylinder was instead exhausted out the chimney on the return stroke of the crankshaft. He introduced the 'compound' whereby a second larger cylinder utilised the excess steam to drive a separate piston. Unfortunately, the engine that Hornblower was trying to develop was worked by a low pressure system and so the addition of a second even lower pressure cylinder had little impact on the engine's working efficiency. In 1804, however, Arthur Woolf took Hornblower's idea and enhanced the effectiveness of an engine worked by high pressure steam, subsequently patenting it the following year.

Fowler's double-crank compound traction engine featured separate rods connecting each piston to the crankshaft where two individual cranks were set at 90 degrees to each other. On every revolution of the crankshaft, four efficient power strokes could now be attained but this complicated and expensive arrangement did not attract as many orders as Fowler had hoped.

In 1889, Burrell patented a single-crank compound locomotive which would prove to be a more successful, affordable and simplistic compromise. With just a single crank, only two power strokes could be achieved but this was still a lot more efficient than the single cylinder engines.

steel plating that largely replaced wrought iron as a build material addressed to a greater extent the weight issue, but engines continued to be constructed ad hoc with the customer's needs very much in mind. Components were built to last although they could still fail and as there was rarely an off-the-shelf spare parts service from the manufacturer, it was usually down to the local blacksmith to fabricate a replacement.

In 1878, the rules governing a vehicle to be escorted by a man carrying a red flag were relaxed allowing local authorities to determine the best policy for their own districts. Greater development in locomotives destined for the home market could now be undertaken by engineering manufacturers. In the 1880s, Fowler and Burrell looked for ways to improve the traction engine's steam efficiency. Fowler adopted a double crank compound system whilst Burrell went for a single crank compound.

By the 1890s, expansion of the rail network across Britain had significantly slowed and traction engines found favourable use in important and

everyday tasks from agricultural needs and industrial work to delivery duties, carrying goods from the railway yard or factory to the door.

The Locomotives on Highways Act (or Emancipation Act) of 1896 and the 1903 Motor Car Act would mark a turning point in the fortunes of the traction engine as they increased the maximum speed allowed for light vehicles and revoked the necessity for a crew of three to accompany a locomotive, another rule stipulated in the 1865 Act. It also abolished, once and for all, the requirement of a man with a red flag preceding a vehicle moving on the highway. Wagons and light tractors could now be employed on door-to-door duties as they were fast, economical and were designed to be driven by one person. Leyland and Thorneycroft were early exponents of the wagon – forerunner to the modern day delivery van – and Messrs Mann and Charlesworth of Leeds showed their entirely new concept 'Steam Cart' at the 1898 Royal Agricultural Show, Birmingham. In a time when any company mass-producing a reliable and powerful internal combustion engined

ABOVE
Portable engine
driving several
machines on
a building site,
c.1911. *(National
Motor Museum/
MPL)*

lorry had yet to be established, little steam tractors of typically seven tons or less, scurried along both rural and urban roads hauling trailers loaded with coal, hard core, timber, hay and even goods such as furniture and removals.

Around the turn of the 20th Century when the horse was rapidly being replaced as a form of motive power,

fair and circus operators up and down the country were purchasing large showman's locomotives that could each substitute for a team of horses, and pull several packing or living vans with ease. The arrival of these beautifully painted and ornately decorated vehicles would be a major event in any village and their annual visit was eagerly anticipated.

ABOVE
W. Tasker &
Sons light tractor
and trailer
outside the Anna
Valley Works,
Andover.
(Image:
Hampshire
Museums
Service)

Likewise, a pair of ploughing engines coming to work the fields would often draw a sizeable and interested crowd. These machines were to be found travelling from farm to farm and following a specific seasonal circuit as not only were they used to till the ground, but also found favour with landowners for such purposes as dredging ponds, lakes and the occasional river.

Where outsized objects could not be carried by rail due to the restrictions imposed by the railway's loading gauge, it was the task of the heavy haulage locomotive or indeed a team of locomotives to move these colossal loads.

From The Ashes...

With advances in development of the internal combustion engine, the traction engine's working days were sadly but inevitably numbered. The effort and time it took to raise steam and prepare an engine at the start of any given day was incomparable to the ease with which a starting handle could throw a motor into life. Additionally, if one looks at the general layout of a typical steam wagon, for example, a relatively small loading bay at the rear was the consequence of as much as half of the vehicle being occupied by boiler, engine, driving compartment and coal bunker compared to the compact cab of a motor lorry.

Between 1880 and 1902, however, discontent over British rule in the Transvaal region of Southern Africa led to civil unrest amongst the Dutch settlers and during the subsequent war with the Boers, traction engines were much in demand hauling vital military supplies and heavy artillery equipment. But in 1911, a national subsidy scheme was introduced where motor lorries could be bought individually or in fleets with the proviso that if any military campaign entailed extra transportation, owners were required to relinquish their vehicles up to 48 hours after notification. Many operators plumped for the scheme though circumstances in Europe during World War I almost immediately called for owners to surrender their vehicles for frontline use. The United States assisted Britain with the war effort by importing thousands of heavy motor vehicles and when war eventually ended, Government depots were able to sell off surplus lorries at very attractive prices. The abundance and choice on offer pretty much spelt the end for less efficient steam-powered vehicles and when several years later repercussions from the Wall Street Crash affected the world's financial organisations, orders unavoidably fell further.

It was a telling time when in 1932, Foden Ltd of Sandbach, once world leaders for the manufacture of steam

wagons, launched a series of motor lorries. One of the Foden family, Edwin, had broken away two years earlier and was already developing a range of internal combustion engined commercial vehicles with his own newly formed company, E.R.F.

Foden's great rivals, the Shrewsbury firm of Sentinel, proudly soldiered on with the first 'Super' type wagon rolling off the production line in 1933 but they too would soon follow suit. For the British market, Sentinel steam wagons only lasted another six years but were still exported in very small numbers up until the late 1940s.

The practicality of the general purpose and agricultural engine was

FROM THE ASHES

RIGHT
Matthew's Yard,
Finchdean
in 1950 with
three derelict
showman's
tractors
and Allchin
agricultural
locomotive
No.1460.
*(National Motor
Museum/MPL)*

gradually overshadowed by an influx
of easier to maintain paraffin tractors
and in an attempt to stave off the
competition, Aveling & Porter Ltd,
Charles Burrell & Sons Ltd, and Richard
Garrett & Sons Ltd, collaborated
to form Agricultural and General
Engineers. Aveling tried to implement
mass-produced parts so that spares could
be more readily available but it was all
just a little too late. A merger between
Barford Brothers, Ruston & Hornsby
Ltd, Ransomes, Sims & Jefferies Ltd
and Aveling & Porter Ltd, eventually
saved the fortunes of those companies
by forming Aveling-Barford Ltd, but for
Burrell and Garrett it was the end of the
road and both companies went out of
business in 1932.

The Road Traffic Act of 1930 was
notable for introducing the driver's
licence, the driving test and *The
Highway Code*, but it also gave greater
power to local authorities to restrict
the axle weight allowed on roads and
bridges. Some traction engines, fully
laden, could weigh more than twenty
tons and the new limitations were an
effective way of reducing the number
of heavy locomotives and encouraging

ABOVE
1937 Sentinel
S4 No.9293 at
the 2008 Great
Dorset Steam
Fair.

the use of motor lorries. Many wagons and traction engines made their final journey to the scrapyard for cutting up, but for the steam roller, the future remained positive and they were used right up until the 1960s with one or two still performing road surfacing duties a decade later. Indeed the M1,

Britain's first motorway, saw Wallis & Steevens 'Advance' rollers employed on its construction.

Although portable engines were still very much in demand for the overseas market, the scrap drive for raw material so essential during the dark days of World War II signalled the final demise of the working steam road locomotive.

The Talyllyn Railway in Gwynedd, Wales is acknowledged as being the first railway preservation society to be founded anywhere in the world. On the 14th May 1951, the inaugural train left Tywyn Wharf Station for Rhydyronen and sparked an obsession among other steam enthusiasts to rescue picturesque and historically important rail routes not only around the country but also around the world.

FROM THE ASHES

Almost a year earlier on the 30th July 1950, Arthur Napper, owner of 1902 Marshall traction engine No.37690, *Old Timer*, wagered he could win a race against Miles Chetwynd-Stapylton and his 1918 Aveling & Porter traction engine No.8923, *Ladygrove*, at Appleford in Oxfordshire. The prize, a firkin (nine gallons) of ale, was duly won by Napper. Further races, attracting the attention of the national press and a crowd of interested onlookers, are now celebrated as the beginning of the preservation movement for steam road-going vehicles. Pathé News filmed the 1952 event and briefly featured another competitor, the 1913 Wallis & Steevens Expansion engine *Pandora* illustrated on an earlier page. *Old Timer* is still an occasional attendee on today's rally circuit but, unfortunately, *Ladygrove* was last registered in 1952 before she was sold for scrap.

Awareness and appreciation for the steam preservation movement have from time to time been boosted by feature films and TV programmes.

T.E.B. Clarke wrote the story for the 1953 British comedy film, *The Titfield Thunderbolt*, and is said to have

FROM THE ASHES

drawn inspiration from the efforts of the Talyllyn Railway Preservation Society. The plot revolves around the villagers of Titfield trying to keep their branch line running. They face stern opposition from an unscrupulous bus operator who, at one point, tries to obstruct train services by persuading a steam roller driver, played by Sid James, to block the track with his engine. The roller in question was 1904 Aveling & Porter R10 No.5590 which at the time of filming was still working and under the ownership of Barnes Brothers of Trowbridge. It was later preserved and now sports the name *Maid Marion*.

In 1962, another British film *The Iron Maiden* was released and followed the efforts of a supersonic aircraft designer, Jack Hopkins, played by Michael Craig, to get his beloved showman's engine to a steam rally at Woburn Abbey. Prior to filming, this engine, Fowler Class R3 No.15657 of 1920, carried the name *Kitchener*. Built as a heavy haulage locomotive, she spent much of her early working life moving blocks of quarried stone on the Isle of Portland, Dorset before returning to the Fowler works in Leeds for alteration into

showman's engine form. Since filming, she has retained a dual personality and *The Traction Engine Register* lists her as *Kitchener/The Iron Maiden*.

In terms of publicising in televisual form the steam preservation scene, chronicling the history of steam power and explaining its effects on industry, nobody generated as much interest as the late Fred Dibnah. The 1979 British Academy Award winning BBC documentary, *Fred Dibnah: Steeplejack* and a subsequent series, *A Year with Fred* followed his fortunes whilst working as a steeplejack. Between demolishing factory chimneys and maintaining church towers in and around his home town of Bolton, Fred was shown driving his 1912 Aveling & Porter 12-ton roller No.7632 *Betsy*, and restoring another Aveling of 1912, KND Class convertible traction engine No.7838. In more recent times, he presented *Fred Dibnah's Industrial Age*, *Age of Steam*, and *The Building of Britain* extolling the country's architectural and engineering heritage, and for all his efforts was awarded an MBE in the 2004 New Years Honours List.

The Portable

O ne of the earliest forms of mass-produced steam-powered machinery that today is included under the 'traction engine' terminology was the 'portable'. As the name suggests, portables were designed to be moved when and where they were needed and, with shafts or harness rings attached to a swivelling front axle carriage, could be pulled along from place to place by one or a team of cart horses depending on size and weight of engine. They were used to drive all manner of machinery, from saw benches and stone crushers to threshing drums and cider presses. The tasks were largely dependent on the seasons so that a portable shared between several farms or estates made good economic sense throughout the year. The majority of portables were fitted with very tall chimneys that could be folded down when in transit. The advantage of height when the chimney was positioned in the upright could, to a certain extent, prevent sparks coming to rest on the predominantly combustible raw materials, such as hay or timber, being processed at the time.

The first recorded use of steam-powered machinery on any farm in Britain was in 1798, this being a stationary engine and essentially fixed in one strategic location. Many farms especially the larger estates had employed stationary engines for various tasks but the limitations were fairly obvious in that crops or foodstuff requiring any form of processing had to be transported

to the engine. Stationary engines by their immense weight and immovability were completely inappropriate for the ploughing of fields for example, and although railway locomotives and steam road vehicles had been developed quite

successfully by the first quarter of the 19th Century, engineers were slow to make the stationary-type engine mobile.

It was not until the 1840s that a number of small engineering firms were experimenting with steam locomotives designed to be moved from farm to farm, so that within a syndicate costs of running and maintenance could be shared, with an overall saving on manpower.

It is generally accepted that in 1841, the Ipswich firm of Ransome were the first to create a stationary-type locomotive mounted on a purpose-built four-wheel chassis and ready for mass-production. In the same year, however, Dean of Birmingham, and Howden and Tuxford, two firms from Boston, Lincolnshire had all unveiled similar alternatives. Unfortunately, there appear to be no surviving portables of Dean and Howard, but Ransome are well represented in preservation with 6, 8, 10 and 12nhp examples. The few diminutive Tuxfords that still exist really illustrate how steam mechanisation could help farming and industry at various levels – all examples of restored Tuxfords rated at just 1 or 1½nhp.

LEFT
This 1906 Robey worked on a sheep shearing station in Australia before restoration and repatriation to Britain.

It seems that of all the counties in Britain to embrace mechanisation for agricultural use, it was Lincolnshire that led the way. In 1843, the Royal Agricultural Society of England reported that several contractors had set up in the county to provide mobile threshing services using portable engines.

The business partnership of Nathaniel Clayton and Joseph Shuttleworth was established in the city of Lincoln during 1842. Ideally situated to observe developments from other manufacturers in the area, Clayton,

'Nhp' or 'nominal horse power' was an antiquated and quite crude method of determining the strength of a locomotive compared to the approximate number of horses needed to perform the same level of work. It was generally calculated by the diameter of the cylinder divided by 10, but in the case of compound cylinder locomotives, there were variations between the method manufacturers chose to compute the figures resulting in actual disparity between similarly rated engines.

Shuttleworth & Company were able to assess and refine the general layout of the portable resulting in a model they exhibited in 1848. They realised that, unlike a self-propelled traction engine, the crankshaft, flywheel and other workings did not need to be anywhere near the rear wheels which were not required to be driven. By placing all motion about-face with the crankshaft and flywheel on the boiler near the chimney and the pistons mounted on the smokebox, the person operating the engine was nearly always at a safe distance away from any potentially dangerous moving parts.

The weight of the portable was kept to a minimum, aided by the omission of any water tank. Instead, feed pumps were fitted and driven off the crank shaft to draw up water from a separate tank or barrel placed alongside.

Not only were portables used for agricultural or light industrial

ABOVE
Savage lighting set bought by Anderton & Rowland in 1900 to power their Electric American Bioscope.

THE PORTABLE

RIGHT
At the 1967
Goodey's Sale,
this Marshall
12nhp made just
£60. *(National
Motor Museum/
MPL)*

application, they also found owners within the entertainment world. Towards the end of the 1800s, fair operators were providing ever larger, more exciting and spectacularly illuminated rides for the pleasure seeking public. In 1900, the well-known West Country showmen, Anderton & Rowland, took delivery of their first steam engine manufactured by Savage Bros Ltd of Kings Lynn. It was specially ordered to power a new element to their travelling show, the Electric 'American' Bioscope, displaying moving pictures to the spellbound audiences. Gradually more and more rides were becoming increasingly sophisticated and it was soon a necessity to invest in an accompanying portable.

Out of all the various traction engine types, the portable remained in production the longest with export models being manufactured right up to the 1960s. But because of the inability to propel itself, the type did not initially find as many enthusiasts in the preservation movement. In time, however, portables have become highly sought after, especially the early models, as they are ideal for demonstrating vintage farm and industrial machinery.

General Purpose
& Agricultural

With the advent of the portable engine, agricultural and industrial work was made considerably easier and more profitable, but to get a portable and any associated machinery to wherever they were needed, the horse was still heavily relied upon for haulage. When J. R. & A. Ransome unveiled the first self-propelled traction engine in 1842, it paved the way for a form of motive power that could easily pull heavy-duty machinery along the road and into position before operating them. The early engines still needed horsepower to steer them although pioneering engineers such as Thomas Aveling and Nathaniel Clayton would, in time, introduce various ideas of steering linkage that could be manually-operated, initially from a platform in front of the smokebox, but

subsequently and almost universally adopted at the rear from the tender.

In 1849, Ransome (which had become Ransome and May in 1846) marketed the 'Farmer's Engine', built by E. B. Wilson & Co. of Leeds. This followed a design similar to that which would later become the standard traction engine layout albeit void of any flywheel. It was intended that on arrival at its place of operation, the Farmer's Engine would either require jacking up so that the rear wheels could power machinery via a belt or, alternatively, a direct drive shaft could be attached to the end of the crankshaft. Like many early locomotives, the Farmer's Engine was a development of the light portable and the resulting lack of weight effectively hampered sufficient haulage capabilities over soft ground.

Experiments in track-laying wheels

GENERAL PURPOSE & AGRICULTURAL

RIGHT
1883 McLaren
7nhp traction
engine No.163
towing another
McLaren, No.60
of 1879.

saw inventor James Boydell design a system whereby pivoting iron shoes positioned at equidistance around a wheel would interlock immediately before contact with the ground. Once in this position, the shoes were creating a continuous flat surface for the wheels to grip and which Boydell referred to as a 'Railway'. Marketed under the name Boydell & Glaisher, his locomotives were, apart from the patent wheels, almost entirely built by other manufacturers – initially Richard Bach in 1855 and Richard Garrett & Sons in 1856, but later by various other firms including Clayton & Shuttleworth. Charles Burrell's exhaustive testing of Boydell's idea attempted to solve the wheel's Achilles heel which was the apparent inadequate strength of each shoe, especially their pivoting hinge, to withstand the harsh pounding received on the poorly maintained roads of the day. If this problem could have been resolved, the system might have seen extensive use especially by the military as there are reports of one locomotive successfully hauling a 138-ton load on its own.

The solution, however, was simple

– make an ordinary wheel larger and wider so that on soft-going it could sustain greater ground coverage and, by incorporating a uniform tread, achieve better grip. The 1878 Road Locomotive Act would later establish the required width of wheel depending on vehicle tonnage, and stated that driving wheels had to be either smooth soled or shod with diagonal cross-bars extending the full breadth of the wheel. Strict guidelines as to the depth of and space

GENERAL PURPOSE & AGRICULTURAL

America, specifically a lack of suitable fuel for long-distance road locomotives. On the semi-arid plains of Argentine Patagonia very few trees grow, and in the 1800s coal imported mainly from Britain was very expensive. John Head, together with Russian engineer, Casimir Schemioth, successfully developed a locomotive that could burn straw, a commodity in plentiful supply, and the company gained tremendous publicity when examples were demonstrated before Queen Victoria and the Emperor of Russia.

At the 1874 Royal Agricultural Society of England's Bedford Show, Ransome's Strawburner won a silver medal and four years later a gold medal at the Paris International Exhibition.

Many manufacturers of locomotives intended for steam cultivation set up their engineering works within agricultural communities. Indeed certain areas of Britain could almost be demarcated by the patronage of owners to their local engine manufacturer. An identifying trademark for all engine builders was the design and embellishment of the flywheel which for general and agricultural purposes all

LEFT
A common sight during the late 1800s was an agricultural engine working out in the fields and operating a threshing set. *(Image: Hampshire Museums Service)*

between each tread were also included.

During the 1870s, Ransomes who, with the appointment of new partner John Head, had become Ransomes, Sims & Head, started tackling a problem often encountered in parts of South

featured a wide rim to accommodate a machinery drive belt.

Wages for agricultural engine crews were very good compared to other farm labourers, and paid overtime and performance bonuses ensured locomotives were valued by their drivers and kept in prime condition. Even during periods of inclement weather, the crews were given a basic retainer if the engine was not able to operate, but it was nonetheless an arduous way to earn a living. Because of the soft ground conditions often encountered, and in order to keep weight to a minimum, general purpose and agricultural locomotives were rarely provided with any form of canopy protection and crews had to endure the elements from baking sun and howling gales to lashing rain and, occasionally, snow. Travelling by road could also prove a challenging exercise and frequent stops at convenient watering points every five or six miles were necessary to keep the tank and more importantly the boiler topped up. It was not unusual to see a traction engine filling up from a pond, stream or river and not unknown to illegally drain a cattle trough!

The Thetford engineering firm of Charles Burrell & Sons offered a special locomotive more suited to the hilly terrain of regions such as the West Country and mid-Wales. Known as the 'Devonshire' or 'D' type, they were mostly built to lighter weight specification with a width of just 6ft 3in to cope with narrow lanes and tracks.

For manufacturers of general purpose locomotives, the early years of the 20th Century were financially rewarding as these engines were popular on large estates where tasks requiring steam operation were numerous and varied. Compared to other traction engine types, they were easy to maintain on a daily basis, relatively cheap to buy and many companies even organised hire purchase schemes to protract the cost of buying from new.

In the 1900s, there were also significant developments in the internal combustion-engined tractor, especially in America. In Britain, engineers were slow to embrace the new technology and only Daniel Albone of Biggleswade made any real progress with his Ivel tractor marketed from 1902. Demonstrated that year in

ABOVE
1908 Foster
general purpose
locomotive
No.3710,
Phoenix.

front of a group of invited guests and dignitaries, the Ivel coped admirably, tilling with relative ease the ground of a rain-sodden field near Old Warden. Among the interested supporters of

the new technology were The Duke of Bedford and the Hon. John Scott Montagu, and Ivel Agricultural Motors Ltd boasted well-known racing drivers, Charles Jarrott and S.F. Edge, on the

Board of Directors. Most early internal combustion engined tractors were not particularly reliable which in part was due to substandard fuel, and for the time being steam cultivation remained relatively unchallenged. Yet the disadvantages of the steam powered vehicle, notably the rudimentary preparation before a day's work, were clear and there for all to see.

Marshall, Sons & Co. Ltd were a traditional engineering firm who in 1848 founded The Britannia Works in Gainsborough, Lincolnshire to make agricultural machinery. In the latter part of the 19th Century they were also proficient builders of steam engines but in 1908 were one of the first large scale manufacturers to turn their skills to an internal combustion engined tractor, with the petrol-paraffin fuelled 'Colonial'.

During World War I, tractors were shipped across the Atlantic from the United States to aid Britain's essential agricultural production and when war ended they were a common sight up and down the country. America was leading the way and affordable tractors from companies such as Fordson, International Harvester and John Deere,

LEFT
The atmosphere at the 2010 Beaulieu Steam Revival is captured nicely with Ransomes, Sims & Jefferies No.39127, *General Wolfe*, making its way up Chestnut Avenue.

alongside examples made in this country including Herbert Austin's small and neat 'R' Type would eventually make the labour intensive traction engine redundant. During the 1920s and '30s,

ABOVE
(Image: Hampshire Museums Service)

RIGHT
Forager, a 1910 Wallis & Steevens 6nhp Expansion Engine No.7155, now owned by Bob Newman of Hampshire.

traction engines could still be seen hard at work but further advances in mechanisation and yet another war in Europe would seal their fate. Even road roller stalwarts Aveling & Porter had successfully turned their hand to diesel tractor development. In 1931, they won a silver medal at the Royal Agricultural Show, Warwick, with their 22/38hp model and in the same year set a world record with a similar example working non-stop for 997 hours. By the 1940s, an agricultural locomotive still in daily use was quite a rarity and all but a few landowners had made the transition to internal combustion power.

Ploughing The Land

Once the power of steam had been harnessed, there was a determination to use it to aid or replace time-consuming and labour intensive processes, none more so than ploughing by horse power. But it was not until the 1830s that a system utilising steam was actually recorded in operation when John Heathcoat and Josiah Parkes patented a ploughing machine commonly regarded as the first successful use of steam for tilling soil. The engine itself was an extraordinary contraption and from contemporary drawings is estimated to have measured a colossal 10 feet high, 32 feet in length, and 22 feet across. It consisted of a two-cylinder steam engine cradled in a frame that was suspended from axles at the four corners. Each axle had a set of three 8-foot diameter wheels and the two sets on each side were connected by a continuous track made of wooden planks on heavy canvas, linked together with metal joints. The method of tillage involved gradually moving the engine across the centre of a field which in turn hauled two ploughs (one on either side) by rope cable between winding drums on the engine and mobile anchor points at the edge of the field. Unfortunately during a public demonstration at the 1837 Highland and Agricultural Society Trials, Dumfriesshire, it is said to have suffered such technical and mechanical failures that it was simply abandoned in the marshland. Relying on seven men to operate the huge beast, the Heathcoat and Parkes steam plough was not considered to be especially cost effective and there, it seems, the project ended.

Development moved to British Guiana where sugar estates in Demerara were about to benefit from steam cultivation. Alexander MacRae and John Osborn worked independently to devise alternative cable operated systems that necessitated the steam engine to be installed on a canal barge. MacRae's idea employed a single engine on one barge and an anchor point on another, the two barges positioned in parallel

canals bordering the plantation and slowly moved alongside the field, pulling the plough back and to between them. Osborn chose instead to use a pair of engines on each side and brought the idea back to Britain where it stirred considerable interest in the agricultural and engineering communities.

John Fowler of Wiltshire began his engineering career in 1847 by joining the Middlesbrough firm of Gilkes, Wilson, Hopkins & Co. as an apprentice. At the time, Ireland was suffering the effects of the potato famine and in 1849, a delegation from the Darlington-based Society of Friends, into which Fowler had been readily accepted, was sent over to try and help. It was from his experiences on this expedition, that Fowler recognised the enormous value of mechanisation in speeding up cultivation processes including field tillage and drain laying. He realised that much of the bog and marshland in Ireland could be made more fertile with adequate drainage, and over the next five years published a number of methods to achieve this, principally variations on the tried and tested systems incorporating cables and pulleys and powered by a single engine.

In 1856 Fowler patented the first purpose-built ploughing engine to feature a gear-driven winding drum, and commissioned two examples from his close associates, Ransomes & May. Also in 1856, he exhibited another innovation, the balance plough, an

ABOVE
Howard double
drum ploughing
engine No.110
of 1876 is one
of only two
known surviving
locomotives from
this Bedfordshire
manufacturer.

implement which could be hauled across a field in either direction without any need to turn it for the return journey. The following year, Fowler experimented with John Osborn's idea of a pair of engines, each positioned at either side of a field hauling a balance plough between them. Frustratingly, recurrent problems caused by rope slack and the additional cost of the second engine encouraged Fowler to withhold this method for the time being.

Seeking a way to adequately replace the horse-drawn plough had, by the late 19th Century, become serious business. At the 1857 Royal Agricultural Society of England Meeting in Salisbury, four competitors were judged on the

ABOVE
One of the
mammoth Z7
type Fowlers,
this example
dates from
1922 and was
displayed at the
1983 Stourpaine
Bushes Rally.

performance of their designs. The first test involved the different locomotives being timed from leaving a yard and reaching the top edge of a steep inclined field, having negotiated a perilous zigzagging track. James Boydell's Burrell fitted with his patent 'Railway' wheels was the only participant to successfully complete the ascent unaided. Collinson Hall's Burrell met with an accident and the two other engines, entered by John Fowler and John Allin Williams, also encountered difficulties. Onto the ploughing itself and the only competitor demonstrating a system using a pair of locomotives that Fowler had, the year previously, chosen to disregard was John Allin Williams. But, as with Fowler's

own trials, Williams' ploughing set proved unsatisfactory and it was possibly the public humiliation of this test that finally got the better of him. The judges reported that his unpleasant behaviour and use of appalling language towards them had made their job practically impossible and his discourtesy was of "a manner they never before had occasion to experience at the meetings of the Society"!

By 1860, John Fowler had reverted back to using a set of two engines per plough and through tremendous publicity boosted by successes in many agricultural competitions, had amassed enough interest and orders to begin building his own steam engines. In partnership with engineer William Hewitson, John Fowler & Company started manufacturing ploughing engines that over the next seventy or so years would largely remain, for all intents and purposes, unchanged in design until they were phased out in the 1930s with the influx of motor tractors.

Ploughing engines fitted with winding drums would typically work in pairs, and often travel from farm to farm and village to village working the

PLOUGHING THE LAND

land following a regular annual circuit. The obvious difference between a ploughing engine and a general purpose or agricultural engine was the size. A larger boiler and tender meant the ploughing engine could remain out in the field much longer before another refill of water or coal was required, and wide wheels front and back prevented the locomotive from sinking into soft ground. The winding drum attached under the boiler was driven by separate gearing from the crankshaft and could be used not only to haul ploughs, but also a variety of other useful implements.

Indeed a pair of Fowler Class AA7 locomotives, No.15364 *Windsor* and No.15365 *Sandringham*, continued to perform contract work using a drag bucket to dredge lakes in various parts of the country, and steadfastly refused to retire. In 2010 they finally ceased earning their keep, joining the steam collection of the Claude Jessett Trust, East Sussex.

The vast majority of ploughing engines preserved in this country were built by John Fowler & Co. (Leeds) Ltd during a period when they were regarded as the very best in the world. At the time of writing, there were 165 surviving examples listed in *The Traction Engine Register*. Fowler were the foremost ploughing engine constructor of their day although there are preserved engines by other manufacturers including those by Burrell, McLaren, Ruston & Hornsby and Aveling & Porter. By comparison, however, and to give some idea as to the extent Fowler dominated the ploughing market, *The Traction Engine Register* numbers these other examples at just sixteen in total!

The Big Guns

The heavy haulage road locomotive (and its flamboyant showman's variant) tend to be the most celebrated type of traction engine and, in terms of monetary value, the most sought after. The highlight of any steam rally is a demonstration of the immense power these incredible machines possess. There is no greater sight than a one-hundred ton trailer load creeping up an incline headed by four hissing and straining heavy haulage engines with two more pushing at the back, exhausts barking in unison and belching plumes of black smoke high into the air. A string of engines undertaking such tasks was not an uncommon sight in 1900s Britain, especially around the major industrial and dockland areas of Cardiff, Glasgow, London, Liverpool and Manchester. How spectacular it must have been to see these engines labouring through the city streets, pulling the turbine, the ship's propeller, railway locomotive or an equally colossal weight that once would have regularly emerged from Britain's world-famous engineering factories.

In 1878, the rules governing a vehicle to be escorted by a man carrying a red flag were relaxed, allowing local authorities to determine the best policy for their own districts. Up until then, locomotive manufacturers had relied on export sales to countries where such stringent rules and regulations were not in place. In the early years of experimentation when the conventional traction engine layout had yet to be settled upon, heavy haulage locomotives proved very useful to those wishing to explore uncharted land such as India's inner territories. Before the arrival of the railway in India, much of the previously inaccessible land was opened up with engines pulling both passenger and freight road trains. One of the pioneers for this market was R. W. Thomson of Leith whose curious looking machine featured a vertical boiler containing tubes that extended down into a 'coffee pot' sat

within the firebox, providing steam
for the duplex engine (two cylinders
of identical diameter taking the same
amount of pressure from the boiler).
Thomson's steamers were distinctive
for their three-wheel arrangement with
the rear driving axle fitted with his own
'resilient wheels'. These were of a type
similar to Boydell's track laying wheels,
but with tyres shod with solid rubber

that could return a very capable speed
of 25mph along the unpaved roads of
India. Thompson only built a handful
of locomotives, choosing to license
production to other companies such as
Burrell, Ransomes and Robey. Another
was Tennant & Co., also of Leith, who
constructed the Thompson-type steamer
between 1867 and 1872.

Before the days of road-building

techniques using hot material, long-distance heavy haulage locomotives had to contend with uneven, rutted and unpaved highways, and were provided with large diameter rear wheels and sprung axles to tolerate the adverse conditions. The considerable mileage sometimes covered in a single journey meant water consumption was notably more than a general purpose engine, for example, and to avoid frequent replenishing stops, they were fitted with a large belly tank in addition to the tender tank. Single-cylinder engines were not as economical for heavy haulage work and most operators chose the compound type offered by various manufacturers. Multiple gearing allowed higher speeds to be attained with motion concealed behind metal panelling to prevent passers-by being coated in lubricating oil and unnerving any livestock close by.

A road locomotive could be made even more useful with the provision of a crane attached ahead of the smokebox. This was driven either via shaft and gearing off the main crankshaft, or through a smaller and entirely separate engine mounted

alongside or in front of the chimney. The length of jib in addition to that of the locomotive itself, however, necessitated careful manoeuvring with drivers forced to take into consideration the limitations in turning circle as well as height restrictions.

The heavy haulage locomotive not only found use in industrial surroundings but was also adopted by the military for moving supplies and artillery. The first 'steam sapper', as these versions came to be known, was commissioned by the government in 1869 following a graphic demonstration of the traction engine's haulage capabilities during that year's Easter Volunteer Review in Dover. Two brand new Aveling & Porter locomotives destined for overseas customers were lent to the military and drew a battery of guns from Dover Railway Station and on up Castle Hill.

The French trialled steam traction for munition haulage in the 1870s and Avelings were sent to Russia in 1876 for testing at the Krasznoje-Selo camp, St Petersburg. This was a very successful exercise and the Russian military ordered several locomotives from the

LEFT
1868 Road
Steamer by R. W.
Thompson, Leith.
(National Motor
Museum/MPL)

THE BIG GUNS

ABOVE
An Indian road train hauled by a Thompson steamer.
(National Motor Museum/MPL)

RIGHT
1910 Burrell 7nhp crane engine No.3197 *Old Tim.*

Rochester Works, subsequently using them to effect in the Russo–Turkish War, a conflict fought between the Ottoman Empire and the Eastern Orthodox coalition from 1877 to 1878. With unrest escalating in the Transvaal region of Southern Africa, armour plated haulage engines operated by the British were particularly effective during the conflicts leading up to and including the Boer War.

Back home, contractors set up businesses to handle the movement of outsize items too large to carry by rail or canal. Companies such as Norman E. Box, Pickfords and Wynns became household names due to the inconceivable feats of transportation they proved were possible time and time again.

The Monmouthshire firm of Robert

THE BIG GUNS

Wynn & Sons established themselves as hauliers in 1863 serving businesses in and around Newport and the Welsh Valleys. Initially, they relied quite literally on horse power for much of their work and continued this practice right up to World War II. Indeed, by 1895, the stables were home to some 200 horses, used in teams to haul a variety of heavy loads such as flour and timber, iron and (later) steel, and all manner of goods from Newport Docks. In 1890, Wynns commissioned a boiler wagon to be built capable of carrying 40 tons. Pulling this required a string of 48 horses in six rows of four. The incredible amount of time, effort

ABOVE Fowler armoured road locomotive hauling munitions/personnel wagons and gun carriages.
(National Motor Museum/MPL))

TRACTION ENGINES

RIGHT

Former Wynns
Fowler A9 class
compound road
locomotive
No.15463,
Dreadnought,
Barry Island
Rally, 1997.

and manpower these operations must have required most likely prompted the company to introduce steam power soon after. A variety of traction engines and wagons came under Wynns ownership until 1930 when legislation in that year's Road Traffic Act reduced the gross weight limit to 24 tons. By then, most of the company's steam vehicles had already been phased out in favour of petrol or diesel engined lorries, the first of which, a 25hp Palladium, was purchased in 1916. A mainstay of the steam fleet, however, was 1920 Fowler A9 7nhp road locomotive No.15463, an engine that has survived into preservation and carries the name *Dreadnought*. Garratt No.33548 was another engine which for many years accompanied the Fowler on numerous tasks including the delivery of contractors' locomotives to the Black Mountains Reservoir construction site at Llanvihangel Crucorney. Wynns also operated Sentinel and Foden wagons, including a versatile timber tractor and an articulated lorry used with flat bed or low loader trailers. Alas none of these or the Garratt appear to have been saved from the scrap man.

The Show
Comes To Town

19th Century Britain was an age when one had to make one's own entertainment. The 'picture house' was yet to be invented, few people could afford to go to the theatre, and social life centred largely around the local pub. Undoubtedly the most eagerly awaited highlight in any village calendar was, therefore, the annual visit from the fair. Packing vans laden with stalls, rides and sideshows pulled by teams of horses would make a grand spectacle, parading onto the village green where camp would promptly be set up. For the next few days, showmen would provide locals with a dazzling display of light, colour and sound, a rare and well earned break from the hardships of work and everyday life.

As the Century progressed, so did the scale and sophistication of fairground rides and larger vans and more horses were needed to cope with the increases. Many travelling companies were not only equipped with all the paraphernalia associated with the fair, but also staged variety shows and some even included a menagerie of wild and exotic animals.

In 1859, American circus proprietor Jim Myers began touring southern Britain and to assist transportation of his show, hired William Bray's agricultural traction engine. This Myers embellished with intricately carved wood painted in bright and attractive colours, a trend emulated by other showmen. Manufacturers eventually adopted the practice around 1910 and the showman-type locomotive, complete with twisted brass, lined out panels and sign-written canopy boards could, thereafter, be ordered straight from the engineering works.

Showman's engines were usually

RIGHT
Former Anderton
& Rowland
showman's
locomotives
(l-r): *Princess
Mary*, *Dragon*,
Earl Beatty,
Queen Mary,
Lord Nelson, *The
Gladiator* and
*White Rose of
York*, Beaulieu
Steam Revival,
2010.

THE SHOW COMES TO TOWN

distinguishable from other types by the full length canopy supported by twisted brass columns, stretching from over the tender at the rear to an extension ahead of the chimney at the front. This extension protected a platform mounted dynamo above the smokebox door that, driven by a belt off the flywheel, could generate more than enough electricity for the largest fairground ride. To

prevent smoke from spoiling the fun of show-goers, an additional stack was carried and could be fitted on top of the chimney, while at the rear some locomotives were provided with crane booms to assist in erecting the rides.

In 1900, one of the largest and most famous shows, run by the West Country family of Anderton & Rowland, had taken delivery of the latest thing, an Electric 'American' Bioscope for the presentation of moving images. To power the arc lighting they purchased a Savage portable steam engine. It made little economic sense, however, to gradually increase the number of horses to pull the show from place to place and in 1905, they replaced the horses and portable engine with three Burrell showman's engines, *The Showman*, *John Bull* and *Jumbo* (later renamed *Unique* and then *Admiral Beresford*). The early showman's engine tended to result from the crude modification of a haulage locomotive yet later in life, many showman's engines were sold off to hauliers again, ending their days moving heavy loads. *The Showman* was one such casualty and having completed four years under Anderton

ABOVE 1921 Burrell Scenic Showman's locomotive No.3912, *Dragon*.

THE SHOW COMES TO TOWN

& Rowland's ownership was stripped of all brightwork and decoration and sold to a mill in Worksop. During the height of their popularity from 1922 to 1938, Anderton & Rowland were operating between six and eight locomotives at any one time. In 1932, they ordered a new engine straight from Fowler's Hunslet Works in Leeds, the 22-ton B6 No.19782, *The Lion*, one of only four of the 'Super Lion' class built, three of which still exist today. This was the second of three Fowlers the family were to own and apart from Tasker showman's tractor, *Marshall Foch*, all their other showman's engines were built by the Norfolk company of Charles Burrell & Sons, Ltd.

Where John Fowler & Co. Ltd specialised in the production of ploughing engines and in later years made a considerable number of road rollers, Charles Burrell & Sons, Ltd were specialists in heavy haulage and showman's locomotives. The Thetford business was originally founded in 1793 by Joseph Burrell who had carried on running his father Benjamin's whitesmith and blacksmith shop to maintain and repair farm implements. On James's death in 1837, his second son, Charles, took over and built the firm into a leading engineering manufacturer employing 400 workers renowned for their high standard of finish. Over the years, all forms of traction engine were offered including portable, general purpose and agricultural, ploughing engines and road rollers. Showmen were particularly attracted to the Burrell locomotive which could be ordered to a fair operator's own specifications with customised decoration, signwriting and livery. In the 1920s, Burrell almost exclusively built the ultimate in showman's engine development called the 'Scenic' in answer to the giant 'Scenic' rides that were at the time being introduced onto the fairground arena. Scenic locomotives were fitted with a secondary dynamo called an 'exciter', located behind the chimney and used to start the ride. But when petrol and diesel tractor units began to permeate the fairground, Burrell's steam business faltered and in 1928, operations were transferred lock, stock and barrel to Richard Garrett and Sons, Leiston.

The last Burrell showman's engine

THE SHOW COMES TO TOWN

RIGHT
The evening showman's engine line-up at the 2010 Great Dorset Steam Fair.

(albeit built by Garratt), was No.4092 *Simplicity* of 1930, an 8nhp three-speed locomotive destined for Alf Deakin & Sons of Brynmawr, Ebbw Vale. In 1934, Deakin also took delivery of, what would turn out to be, the very last showman's engine built in Britain, Fowler No.20223 *Supreme*, another B6 'Super Lion' and sister engine to Anderton & Rowland's *The Lion*. To mark *Supreme's* significance, it was decided to embellish her with chromium brightwork rather than brass. By the 1940s, *Simplicity* and *Supreme* had relinquished their fairground activities and transferred to Clydeside to work for Road Engines & Kerr (Haulage) Ltd. After World War II, both were retired for preservation but their value had yet to be realised and, regrettably, *Simplicity* was scrapped in 1946.

Fortunately *Supreme* and a great many other showman's engines have been lovingly restored and a highlight of the annual Great Dorset Steam Fair is the evening display of locomotives once operated by the likes of Anderton & Rowland, Pat Collins and Charles Thurston, illuminated and lined up in front of the vintage fair.

Delivering
To Your Door

For the carriage and delivery of bulk goods and commodities, the 1870s saw a number of engineering firms such as Brown & May and John Yule experiment with steam 'lurries'. In 1896, a vertical boiler van by John Thornycroft and Colonel Niblett was demonstrated at Kew carrying a half-ton load and four passengers. In the same year other examples were shown by the Lancashire Steam Motor Company, Leyland, and the Liquid Fuel Engineering Co., Ltd, boiler makers from East Cowes on the Isle of Wight. The latter company built the Lifu and in 1898 a passenger service was begun between Fairford and Cirencester using a Lifu van and trailer.

The Light Locomotive Act of 1903 allowed manufacturers more freedom to develop a range of steam wagons and tractors. Speed limits had already been increased in 1896 and rules previously applied to vehicles requiring a minimum number of three crew consisting of driver, steersman and red flag man were relaxed. Locomotives weighing five tons or less could now be operated by just one person.

Builders of steam wagons generally opted for one of two categories – the 'undertype' or the 'overtype', referring to location of the engine.

The engine on an undertype was typically suspended beneath the main vehicle chassis and between the front and rear axles. Representing little more than a development of the horse-drawn dray, early undertypes relied on traditional crafts in their production and among the many manufacturers who for a brief period tapped into the market were the Bristol Wagon & Carriage Works Ltd, H. Carmont of Kingston-

ABOVE
This 1906
St. Pancras
was operated
between
Lymington and
Bournemouth
by J. W. Lance.
*(National Motor
Museum/MPL)*

upon-Thames, the English Steam Wagon Co., Hebden Bridge, and Entwistle & Gass Ltd of Bolton. A curious vehicle to emerge from the early 1900s was the 'Manchester' made by Turner, Atherton & Co., Ltd, Denton. It was simply a two-wheel fore-carriage containing a vertical boiler and engine that could be attached to an existing horse dray thus transforming it into a steam wagon.

Competition from companies specialising in the overtype was too strong for the smaller firms and only a few lasted the distance. The Yorkshire

Patent Steam Wagon Company was one of the success stories, trading from 1900 until the last steam wagon emerged from their Leeds works in the mid-1930s. Yorkshires had a distinctive transverse double-ended boiler where the exhaust gases from the firebox split between two separate smokeboxes before returning to a central header chamber and out through the chimney.

Another company to prosper was the Glasgow engineering firm of Alley & McLellan, established in 1906. This firm led the way in developing the undertype and their 'Sentinel' wagon featured a vertical boiler that heated water in the surrounding jacket as well as tubes passing through the top of the firebox. In a bizarre marketing scheme aimed at discrediting overtype vehicles from other manufacturers, Alley & McLellan also built one example of the overtype in 1911. They claimed that in tests, even their overtype's superior build and running qualities over other makes were no match for their own undertype. The campaign backfired slightly, interest for their overtype was significant, and in the end they were obliged to build sixteen of them! In 1915, a new factory was

set up on the outskirts of Shrewsbury and over the next three years, the entire business was relocated and renamed Sentinel (Shrewsbury) Ltd.

With the undertype's boiler taking up minimum space in the driver's cab and the engine tucked neatly out of the way, a large rear load carrying area was available, but the condition of early 20th Century highways meant

ABOVE
4nhp VB-type compound 5-ton wagon made by E. S. Hindley of Bourton, Dorset.

ABOVE
A Yorkshire
Steam Wagon
loaded with bales
of sheepskin,
c.1905 (National
Motor Museum/
MPL)

the underslung engine was prone to damage from mud, dust and stones. Off road, the exposed cylinders and motion were at even greater risk and many manufacturers chose the overtype as a safer alternative.

The overtype was a direct descendant of the traction engine with crankshaft and cylinder block mounted on top of a locomotive-type boiler.

P. J. Parmiter, an engineer of farm implements from Tisbury, Wiltshire, had designed and patented the 'Steam Cart' and displayed a model of it at the 1886 Norwich Show. But it was not until 1897 that the Leeds firm of Mann & Charlesworth agreed to begin production, unveiling the first

example at the following year's Royal Agricultural Show, Birmingham. It was of a most innovative layout and caused much interest among the show-goers. Intended for one person operation, the driver's footplate was positioned on the offside of the firebox between the wheels, with fire hole and all controls located within easy reach. A large bucket over the rear wheels could be tipped by winding a screw thread and was designed to be completely detachable

from the main engine. Steering was via the conventional traction engine system of worm gear and chain although a subsequent version, entered into the 1901 Liverpool Self-Propelled Traffic Association Trials, had a more direct system of shaft and bevel gears.

A year after Mann & Charlesworth first exhibited their 'Steam Cart', E. Foden, Sons & Company, Sandbach, began experimenting with their own version of the overtype. This was a

LEFT
Foden C-Type Wagon No.13316, *Sir Lionel*, was built in 1929 as a tar tanker.

RIGHT
1919 Mann 'Steam Cart' No.1386, *Brinkburn Lass*.

ABOVE 1928 Foden No.13090 originally left the Sandbach Works as an articulated lorry tractor before conversion to its current guise.

relatively larger vehicle and peculiarly carried the rear axle in outside frames, similar to that on a railway wagon. In 1901, they entered their second prototype in the War Office Trials at Aldershot, its overall performance earning the runners–up prize of £250. The winning vehicle had been entered by the Basingstoke firm of John I. Thornycroft & Co. Ltd but questions were asked over the result and even debated in Parliament as the Foden, on paper, looked a clear victor. Buoyed by their success, however, Fodens went into production and as orders were steadily taken, slight changes could be made to the initial design. In 1904, the

ABOVE
A tractor made
by W. Tasker &
Sons, Andover
demonstrates
the versatility of
these neat little
engines.
(Image:
Hampshire
Museums
Service)

outside frames were dispensed with in
favour of an orthodox leaf-sprung rear
axle, a choice of more powerful engines
and larger capacity flatbed body styles
were added to the range, and as road
surfaces across Britain were beginning
to improve, it seemed appropriate to fit
smaller wheels.

A Foden wagon could travel the
commendable distance of 30 miles on
one tank of water and had coal capacity
for 40 miles. During World War I, all
factory output was intended for military

use with wagons proving indispensable
in moving munition to the front line.
When War ended, cheap surplus
wagons flooded the British market
causing sales problems and a drop in
orders not only for other manufacturers,
but for Foden as well.

In total, some 6,500 examples were
dispatched from Elworth Works between
1900 and 1935 including, from 1927,
a rigid six-wheeler model albeit 24
years after their drawing office had
first penned the idea. In an attempt

to compete with main rivals Sentinel, Foden began building undertypes in 1931 but a year later had succumbed to new technology and started manufacturing motor lorries.

With the exception of a few timber tractors, Sentinel's Shrewsbury based production output was almost exclusively steam wagons of four types: the 'Standard', 'Super', 'DG' and finally the 'S'. They were very popular abroad with many being exported to South America and even built under licence by foreign manufacturers - Skoda, for example, began producing 4, 5, and 6-ton wagons from 1924.

Drive from the crankshaft for either undertype or overtype wagons could be via chain or gearing, although Sentinel introduced the carden (propeller) drive shaft with a conventional lorry rear axle on the 'S' type in the final decade of steam wagon production. With the capability to reach a speed of 60mph, the 'S' was the pinnacle of wagon design and a competent alternative to the

ABOVE
1912 Wallis & Steevens tractor operated by Waring & Gillow Ltd, London. *(National Motor Museum/MPL)*

motor lorry, but due to the time it took to generally prepare and raise steam pressure for a day's work, it would soon fall out of favour with commercial vehicle operators.

In 1949, the last Sentinel steam wagon was dispatched to a customer in Argentina but examples from the Shrewsbury firm continued working for many years after. Some of the earliest 'Standard' types were in use at Brown Bayley Steel, Sheffield, right up to withdrawal in 1970 when they found new owners in preservation.

Foden is well represented today with more than a hundred wagons, tractors and traction engines surviving. A similar number of Sentinels are preserved in Britain but only one example built in Glasgow by Alley & McLellan exists and is displayed at the Grampian Transport Museum, Alford.

The slow demise of the steam wagon was a direct result of the influx and development of the motor lorry, but an even earlier casualty was the light steam tractor, a type that had all but disappeared from British roads by World War II.

Introduced en masse after the 1903 Light Locomotive Act, the tractor was an extremely practical alternative to the wagon and could be put to a number of useful tasks when not on road haulage duties. Aimed at the bulk carrier, tractors of seven tons or less could be found scurrying along the highway pulling trailers loaded with coal, timber, road stone, flour and hay. Tractors were another engine type that could be operated by one person so were economical to run, and healthy competition between manufacturers meant locomotives were generally offered at an attractive price from new. Meager coal and water capacity limited their use over distance but they were ideal for furniture and removal firms such as Waring & Gillow, the Oxford Street furnishers, who used tractors to haul trains of pantechnican vans.

Many showmen took delivery of these little engines to assist with lighter jobs around the fairground, embellishing them with all the finery of their larger showmans engine cousins.

For the preservationist, the tractor represents a compact, manageable and relatively easy-to-maintain traction engine compared to the larger general purpose, agricultural and road locomotives. For this reason alone, steam tractors are just as sought after and command premium prices!

Rolling Stone

Of all the vehicles that can be cloaked under the modern-day interpretation of the term 'traction engine', the humble steam roller is distinct. It was designed to earn its keep unassisted, not to haul heavy loads or carry goods, or even to operate machinery, but simply to scarify the ground, or crush road-building material by its own sheer weight alone and without the use of additional equipment.

In the early 19th Century, British highways and byways were in an appalling state having endured years of pummelling from the solid wheels of carts and carriages, and the incessant churn from horses' hooves. Town and city roads were just as bad, with an almost continual flow of pony traps or cabs and livestock taken to and from the market place. Tentacles of railway lines had connected large areas of country and the speed, efficiency and relative comfort of rail travel had caused any development and improvements in road-building techniques to be neglected.

Dusty and rutted tracks out in the country would quickly become mud filled channels during spells of heavy rain, and reports of impassable routes were widespread.

During the early 1800s, civil engineer Thomas Telford set about re-introducing in rural areas road-making principles that had once been the obsession of Roman settlers fourteen centuries before. The technique involved establishing a bed of large slab stones onto which were laid progressively smaller bands of hard core whilst creating a gentle camber for drainage. An alternative approach was that of John Loudon Macadam who promoted the theory that the longevity of a compacted dirt based road, for example, could be improved with a top layer of uniform broken stones. Any rain water seeping through would, with passing traffic, form a sticky clay to help adhere the stones together creating an even surface. Given those ideas, the advent of heavy haulage locomotives could

not have been welcomed with great enthusiasm. Government legislation and hefty road charges were all intended to reduce the number of vehicle movements – especially in daylight hours – and prevent unnecessary damage to the roads.

In France and Prussia, horse-drawn water-filled rollers had been extensively used to flatten macadam paved roads. Frenchmen, Louis Lemoine and Amedée Jean Ballaison, patented steam powered rollers within a year of each other. Lemoine's ungainly design of 1859 featured a single, centrally-placed roller with two castor-wheel outriggers whilst Ballaison opted for a portable-type engine cradled in a girder frame and supported by tandem rollers at either end. Ballaison's machine was recommended by advisors to the French Government but both designs were noted as a vast improvement to horse-drawn rollers.

Thomas Aveling had also recognised that the wheels of haulage locomotives combined with their immense axle weight could be beneficial to compacting and levelling any loose material, and he set out to win over the

critics – after all, business was business and his at that time was in heavy road locomotive construction!

Aveling's first experiment in roller design was to take a standard traction engine and equip it with large smooth 3-foot wide wheels of 7-foot diameter. Behind this was attached a trailing drum to flatten any areas the engine had missed. In 1866, a similar device was demonstrated in Hyde Park, London and a year later examples of Aveling's first purpose–built self-contained road roller were delivered to Liverpool Corporation and a customer in France. These were, however, of a most unconventional back to front design similar to a road locomotive introduced in 1863 by William Clark and William Forthergill Batho of Birmingham. Twin trailing rollers, weighted by a 500 gallon ballast tank positioned directly above, were steered by a large ship's wheel from the centrally placed footplate. The front rollers were driven, via a large gear off the crankshaft and heavy chain, by a single-acting 12nhp engine with a cylinder measuring eleven inches in diameter. It weighed a mighty 30 tons and measured over ten feet in width and in an attempt to improve performance, Aveling gradually made several changes to subsequent vehicles, reducing the weight, first to 24 tons and then 15 tons. The central steering position caused visibility problems and Aveling decided to abandon the Batho-type engine completely. Even so, over eighty examples had been made by 1871 mostly exported to either the United States, France or India.

The clumsy handling characteristics found in operating the Batho-type forced Aveling to rethink and revert back to a design more akin to the traction engine. In addition to the smooth rear wheels, he replaced the front wheels with smaller twin rollers thus creating the 'three-point' roller – rollers positioned in three points of contact to the ground with three slightly overlapping lines of track. In utilising the conventional traction engine layout, a driver had far better visibility over the road he was rolling and in financial terms, locomotives could be constructed with the majority of Aveling's existing traction engine components, reducing further tooling costs. They could also, thereafter, be built to more manageable specification and were made available in a choice ranging between 6 and 15 tons.

It was only a matter of time before steam rollers were a commodity common and essential to road builders, and other firms such as John Fowler & Co. Ltd, T. Green & Sons, and John & Henry McLaren Ltd were tapping into the market.

In an effort to provide a more

versatile machine, some manufacturers built 'convertibles', a type that could either be used as a roller or light tractor. A drawback encountered with this idea was that the compromise in gearing was found to be too high for satisfactory rolling and too low for adequate road speed. Subsequently, 'convertibles' proved not as popular as initially hoped.

Early years of development

were naturally and understandably experimental until a three-point roller layout was almost universally elected as the convention for production. New thinking, however, persisted long after the turn of the Century especially when tarmac and bitumen were first used. Crude gas tar to bind top surface road stones had been mooted as far back as the early 1800s and was adopted in

ROLLING STONE

RIGHT
1924 Burrell
Class A roller
No.3991,
Daffodil, at the
2010 Beaulieu
Steam Revival.

France and some parts of the United States soon after. It was not until 1905 that certain counties in England began road improvements using tarmac and with this more sophisticated approach came a necessity for lighter rollers with an even weight distribution. Many towns and cities had also chosen electric tram systems to form the nucleus of their public transport infrastructure and it soon became apparent that there was an unexpected need for narrow steam rollers to pack down the surface between tramway rails. Once more, thoughts turned to the tandem layout first advocated by Ballaison in 1860 but comprising much smaller front and rear rollers, the latter secured on an axle held in a frame and attached to the two tender plates. T. Green & Sons were early proponents of the narrow tandem but production from other manufacturers would continue right up to the mid-1920s, including those from Armstrong-Whitworth Ltd, Marshall, Sons & Co., Ltd and, in particular, Robey & Co., Ltd, whose model range of 5 to 8-ton locomotives were popular with overseas customers.

Some curious variants emerged from Aveling & Porter's Rochester works including, in 1911, a tandem featuring a vertical twin-cylinder engine to the design of American engineer, Ephraim Shay, and mounted on the offside of the locomotive. To counterbalance this, the water tank was sited on the nearside and the omission of any flywheel meant the locomotive could rapidly change direction - a tremendous asset when working with asphalt which prevented the locomotive sinking into the hot molten surface. From 1921, Aveling built a number of vertical boiler (coffee pot) tandems boasting steam power-assisted steering - another innovation to aid quick traversal over soft asphalt.

Conventional heavyweight three-point rollers were somewhat limited to flattening rough foundation hard core, and although using the lighter tandem design was ideal for finishing the top layer of tarmac, they were, because of the narrow track, found to be time consuming and relatively unstable. Engineering firms steadily worked towards a compromise but it was not until 1923, that the greatest steps in steam roller design were taken by the Basingstoke company

of Wallis & Steevens Ltd when they introduced the 'Advance'. Before then, Wallis & Steevens traction engine production, almost entirely aimed at the agricultural sector, was stoically workmanlike but quite unremarkable compared to their many adversaries. The 'Advance', however, combined attributes from both the conventional heavy three-point roller and the light and narrow tandem. The 'Advance' embraced practical knowledge with new thinking, and can be considered as the true forerunner to the modern motor road roller. Powered by a duplex engine, it comprised no heavy flywheel so was capable of performing the rapid reverse operation that Aveling's Shay had

ABOVE 1912 Marshall 10-ton 4nhp convertible No.60207, *Tutor*.

ROLLING STONE

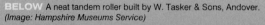

ABOVE 1930 Robey tri-tandem roller No.45655, *Herts Wanderer* on the Lamerton to Tavistock road in 1996.

admirably demonstrated. The rear rollers could independently follow the angle of a road camber due to an ingeniously designed rear axle and the sizes of the front and rear rollers were equalised to impart similar downward pressure onto the road surface. Constant weight distribution was significantly improved by twin coal bunkers placed each side of the driver's footplate and the water tank was relocated to form pannier tanks either side of the boiler. Intended to be operated by one man, some features peculiar to the 'Advance' took some getting used to especially a horizontally mounted steering wheel located next to a smaller but almost identical wheel acting as the steam regulator. The author can verify that to the uninitiated, when you think you are going to steer the engine into a sharp corner, you are in fact about to substantially increase your straight line speed – an exhilarating experience, none more so for the instructor stood behind you!

In the 1920s and '30s, an era when many road locomotive operators had already replaced much of their steam powered vehicles with more up-to-date motor lorries, the steam roller

and especially the Wallis & Steevens Advance, of which 272 examples were made, soldiered on and remained in service for many years after World War II. Even though the last British-built steam roller had left the works of Aveling & Barford in 1948, the 'Advance' was still very much in demand right up to the 1960s. Indeed Britain's first motorway, the M1, owes much of its construction to this remarkable machine.

ABOVE 1927 Wallis & Steevens 'Advance' 10-ton roller No.7933.

ABOVE Fowlers, No.9005, *Lord Kitchener*, of 1901 and motor roller No.17954 of 1928.

Odds & Sods

Ever since Richard Trevithick, Goldsworthy Gurney and Walter Hancock had in the 1800s experimented with steam vehicles for the carriage of passengers, several manufacturers flirted with the same idea but competition from the railway network was too great for any noteworthy success. There were examples of Sentinel and Foden steam omnibuses but these were few and far between. The best known and most prominent was perhaps *Puffing Billy*, a bus built specifically to transport the Foden Motor Works Brass Band. Unfortunately, the original no longer exists but replicas have been made and prove popular when ferrying visitors around the various steam events and rally fields.

In an attempt to improve haulage capabilities especially over muddy ground, some engineering companies tried to incorporate four-wheel drive into traction engine design. One of the first was the American firm of Wood, Taber & Morse based in Eaton, Madison County. Their 1884 'Four Driver' had an engine layout similar to the portable with cylinder block close to the driver's footplate, and crankshaft and flywheel at the front near the chimney. The rear wheels were driven through a bank of five large gears, whilst a sixth gear operated a shaft that passed through the perch bracket (the block on which the boiler rests over the front steering axle) to another set of gears propelling the front wheels. Turning of the front steering axle was possible with the inclusion of a universal joint inside the perch bracket. At the 1886 World's Fair, London, their 'Four Driver' won a coveted Blue Ribbon of Excellence and in recent years, an example was displayed at the Henry Ford Museum, Dearborn, Michigan.

At about the same time that the 'Four Driver' was announced, two companies in Britain were also working on four-wheel-drive traction engines. The Durham and North Yorkshire

STEAM POWER

Printed in England © J. SALMON LTD., SEVENOAKS, KENT. TEL: [01732] 452381

Clockwise from top left

1924 Ransomes, Sims & Jefferies Light Agricultural Locomotive
1922 Burrell Showmans Road Locomotive 'Margaret'
1902 Fowler A4 Compound Road Locomotive 'Kitchener'
1920 Ruston & Hornsby Ltd. Traction Engine 'Oliver'
1924 Fowler DN1 10-ton Road Roller 'Highlander'
1914 Burrell Gold Medal Tractor 'Gladstone'

ODDS & SODS

RIGHT
1923 Foden
No.11340 with
replica bus body
participating
in the 1997
London to
Brighton Historic
Commercial
Vehicle Run.

Steam Cultivation Company Ltd had built an engine to a Walter Johnson and Samuel Phillips design using a ball and socket front axle arrangement, whilst Alfred Grieg, Richard Shaw and John Whittingham had collaborated with John Fowler & Co., Ltd to build their version that featured a similar steering system to the Wood, Taber & Morse, albeit with front drive operated via a heavy chain off the crankshaft.

Before the age of the motor tractor, there were two established schools of thought with regard to mechanised ploughing, that of whether to use two steam locomotives positioned either side of a field and hauling a balance plough between them, or to follow horse–drawn practice and drag a plough across the field directly behind a single locomotive. One oddity that has survived into steam preservation is a traction engine designed for direct ploughing built in 1872 by J & F Howard of Bedford. By the 1870s, most manufacturers had adopted the standard locomotive layout of motion and cylinder block positioned on top of the boiler, with a short exhaust pipe venting spent steam from the cylinders to the chimney.

568
JOHN FOWLER & C?
ENGINEERS, LEEDS.

The clean lines of the Howard were achieved by locating the single cylinder low in the tender with its cover plate protruding rearwards from the bunker. With the cylinder in this position, the crankshaft and flywheel required placing low as well and the flywheel could not, therefore, be seen when viewing the locomotive from the offside. It also meant the steam exhaust needed to be routed from the tender and vented through a long pipe under the boiler to the base of the smokebox.

Other manufacturers marketed traction engines for direct ploughing use and the Garrett 'Suffolk Punch' was possibly the most unorthodox. The boiler, turned front to back, had the firebox, cylinder block and steering gear positioned within an open cab above the front axle. The chimney, crankshaft and flywheel were at the back over the driving wheels. Only four were ever made by the firm of which one has survived into preservation.

The Mann 'Steam Cart' was yet another locomotive type used for direct ploughing but which also found employment in a variety of different roles. Light road haulage, goods carrier

ABOVE
1872 Howard 8nhp direct ploughing engine No.201, *Britannia*.

LEFT
The 1885 Whittingham-Fowler A Class four-wheel-drive traction engine. *(National Motor Museum/MPL)*

and even road rolling were some of the tasks gainfully undertaken by this versatile little engine.

The 'Steam Cart' was intended for single person operation, as was the Wallis & Steevens 'Simplicity'. This strange and diminutive machine with its inclined launch-type boiler and twin coal bunkers positioned on top of the belly tank was, at 3 tons, designed for light rolling work such as pavements, driveways and tennis courts. Publicised from 1925, the 'Simplicity' was a late

ABOVE
The last surviving Garrett 'Suffolk Punch' tractor shown attending the 1986 Battersea Park Domesday Fair. This engine, No.33180, is now exhibited at the Garrett Museum, Leiston.

arrival on the steam scene and by that time, petrol engined competition had already made its mark. To be given the name 'Simplicity' might have been a little optimistic as in practice performance proved erratic with difficulty maintaining steam pressure. Not surprisingly, there were few takers and only a dozen or so were completed.

Savages of Kings Lynn were the first manufacturer to build a range of 'showman's centre engines' designed to form part of the structure of a galloper fairground ride. This was an attempt to dispense with the inconvenience of employing a non-self-propelled portable-type centre engine for such work that had, up until then, generally been accepted practice. The showman's centre consisted of tall extensions to the hornplates (the plates that made up the sides of the firebox) to form a lattice frame tower on top of which was mounted the central turntable of the ride. The turntable was set in motion through a series of gears and bevels working separately off the crankshaft. In transit, exhaust from the firebox and cylinders were vented through a conventional locomotive-type chimney but when used for powering the ride, smoke and steam were diverted through an angled flue that passed through the centre of the turntable. This prevented acrid smoke fogging the pleasure seekers! Unfortunately, this type of engine, originally designed for heavy haulage, was considered too powerful and dangerous for the structure of the rides and many locomotives had the latticework superstructure removed and subsequently converted for haulage work only.

Probably the most rakish-looking vehicle made during the heyday

of steam was the Robey Express
Steam Tractor. Largely based on the
company's overtype wagon design,
it also featured a circular firebox and
chain drive, and was capable of attaining
25-30mph hauling bulk loaded trailers.
The first was ordered in 1922 by South

African Railways although it was never
delivered and instead was sold to East
Anglian Roadstone, whilst the last
example was sent to Ceylon in 1934.
Only nine are thought to have been
built and, today, the two that have
survived into preservation date from

ABOVE
1919 Mann
compound light
'patching' roller
No.1145, *Miss
Mann*.

in quarries, lime and cement works but the limitations regarding their haulage capabilities prevented them from being of any benefit to heavier industry. In 1872, the School of Military Engineering at Brompton Barracks took delivery of an Aveling steam sapper that could be converted for rail use. Other manufacturers including Fowler offered similar rail-borne locomotives and several of the Avelings have found their way into preservation.

It is interesting to note that in 1993, whilst excavating the former Brindley Ford Colliery, near Stoke-on-

ABOVE
1927 Wallis & Steevens Simplicity roller No.7936, *Pepperpot*, at the 2009 Welshpool & Llanfair Railway Gala.

RIGHT
Sentinel were another company who produced a neat tractor design with their Super two-speed. This one, displayed at the 2010 Isle of Wight Steam Rally, is No.6426 of 1926, recently repatriated from Australia.

1927 and 1929 respectively.

Between 1867 and 1926 a number of locomotives were dispatched from Aveling's Rochester works, specifically designed to run on industrial and passenger tramways. Several of these resembled little more than traction engines riding on flanged railway wheels, with a large flywheel and motion mounted on top of the boiler. 2-2-0 or 0-4-0 wheel arrangements were available and all were gear or chain-driven off the crankshaft. Many saw service as light shunting engines

Trent, workers unearthed the remains of a chain-driven steam engine, later substantiated to be the oldest Aveling & Porter still in existence and dating from around 1866 or '67. Its origins were still under debate but was likely to have been built as a tram loco and converted to operate a winding drum by the owners of the colliery. Soon after rediscovering the remains, there were plans to use them to recreate a 15-ton Batho-type road roller, complete with ship's wheel, similar to one supplied to the City of Sheffield around 1870.

ABOVE
1900 Aveling & Porter 0-4-0TG No.4780 at Croydon Gas Company. *(National Motor Museum/MPL)*

LEFT
1926 Aveling & Porter 2-2-0TG geared traction railway engine No.9449 at the 2010 Bluebell Railway 50th Celebrations.

Traction
Engines Today

There is something extremely fascinating about a steam engine. A petrol or diesel motor functions by a controlled but particularly ferocious method via means of an explosion of combustible liquid or gas in a cylinder in order to force the movement of a piston. The motion is completely concealed within a block containing other cylinders working on the same principle, which in turn is hidden from view under a cloak of bonnet and bodywork.

A steam engine, on the other hand, is very open with nearly all the workings exposed and is powered by what is essentially, nothing more than vaporised water – albeit at extremely high pressure! Most traction engines work best with a steam pressure of between 150 and 200 pounds

per square inch and the process of achieving that begins with a good fire evenly covering the grate in the bottom of a firebox. A water jacket envelopes the firebox, and within the water filled boiler a series of tubes connect the firebox to the smokebox at the front, on top of which is mounted the chimney.

The water jacket and multi-tube boiler were first introduced in the 1820s by French engineer, Marc Seguin, and the advantage of such an increased surface area heating the water was effectively demonstrated by Stephenson's *Rocket* when it won the Rainhill Trials in 1829. As the fire burns, hot exhaust gases not only heat the water in the jacket, but by passing through the boiler tubes also heat the water surrounding them before the gases are discharged into the smokebox and up out of the chimney.

Steam pressure builds in a confined space in the top of the boiler and only has two ways to escape. The first is through safety valves provided to prevent too much pressure being contained in the boiler, but ultimately to stop the boiler from exploding.

LEFT
Fowler B5 crane engine, *The Great North*, and Burrell road locomotive, *Duke of Kent*.

The second more desirable option is through a series of valves in the cylinder block controlled by the driver using a regulator. The regulator lets steam into the cylinder and the extreme pressure forces a piston to move within the cylinder. Each piston is connected via a rod to a crank on a shaft that is located over the firebox and that also bears a large flywheel at one end. The rotating flywheel aids the smooth reciprocating movement of the piston as it reaches the apex of stroke at either end of the cylinder.

Large cogs link the crankshaft with the rear wheels in order to drive them and performance is determined by the selected gear – low gear for slow work, traversing rough ground and climbing steep inclines for example, and higher gear or gears for a more efficient road run. Out of gear, steam can still be used to pump water from the locomotive's tank to top up the boiler and with a belt driven off the flywheel, it can also be used to operate other machinery such as a saw bench and threshing drum, or in the case of the showman's engine, generate electricity via a dynamo. On locomotives designed for those tasks where an even speed of the crankshaft is required, automatic admission of steam into the cylinder is regulated with the provision of a governor controlled by centrifugal force.

Watching a steam engine ticking over is mesmerising, satisfying and really quite relaxing!

In the austere years following World War II, derelict road locomotives that had somehow avoided the cull of the wartime scrap drive, could be bought at bargain prices. Even showman's engines that

TRACTION ENGINES TODAY

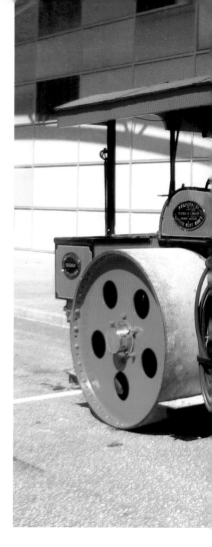

continued to perform sterling work for travelling fair operators were gradually being replaced by ex-military diesel haulage tractors and could be purchased on a fairly reasonable budget. But as enthusiasm grew, and the historical and entertainment value of these machines was progressively realised, so the prices began to escalate and today a showman's engine, for example, will cost hundreds of thousands of pounds to buy. An owner will then spend many hours of hard work and thousands of pounds again keeping it in running order. Luckily, one doesn't have to own a traction engine to enjoy the grace, power and splendour of these marvellous machines and today's rallies are more popular than ever with many locomotives regularly attending.

Museums are also great places to view static exhibits occasionally steamed for demonstration purposes. There are fantastic collections of steam vehicles at Amberley Museum & Heritage Centre, West Sussex, Bressingham Steam Museum, Diss, the Charles Burrell Museum, Thetford, Dingles Steam Village, Lifton, and Milestones in Basingstoke, to name but a few.

The Restoration
Of No.12335

BELOW
Aveling & Porter
No.12335 being
delivered to
Southampton
City Council in
the early 1960s.

In 1929, the Rochester works of Aveling & Porter Ltd dispatched No.12335, a D-Type 8-ton compound piston valve steam roller, to Bridgwater Borough Council, Somerset

and having performed many years of sterling work it was subsequently sold to Eddison Plant Limited.

Frank Eddison began trading from Wareham Road, Dorchester in 1877 after moving his business from Martinstown where it had been established seven years earlier. Eddison Plant Limited was one of a number of firms, operating in the early years of the 20th Century, that hired out heavy plant equipment. Companies such as John Allen & Sons, Oxford, and Messrs Buncombe of Highbridge, Somerset catered for all building requirements, becoming well-known suppliers of heavy duty machinery that included large fleets of steam rollers. Eddison had already set up many yards up and down the country when No.12335 began working in and around the Hampshire town of Romsey.

BELOW
No.12335 showing
how years of abuse
and neglect in the
Millbrook playground
had taken its toll on
the engine with many
parts removed.

In the early 1960s she was superseded by more up-to-date motor rollers and was presented to Southampton City Council for display in Millbrook playground. The roller remained there for nearly thirty years providing entertainment and a climbing frame for many local children but, in the late 1980s, found a new owner and was finally removed on the 3rd December 1987.

Nigel Spender has spent nine years restoring the roller, meticulously returning the locomotive to her former glory. To Nigel's immense credit, it has been a monumental labour of love as many parts, especially those made from bronze or brass, were unceremoniously removed whilst she resided in the playground. Using original works drawings, these have all been faithfully reproduced to Aveling's design in Nigel's spare time and in his own workshop. At the time of writing, most of the work had been completed and after more than fifty years it was planned that No.12335, sporting the name *Hilda*, would steam once again in 2011.

ABOVE No.12335 after removal for restoration.

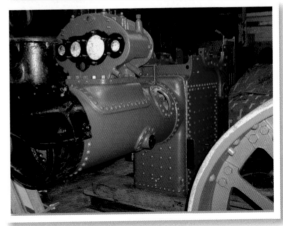

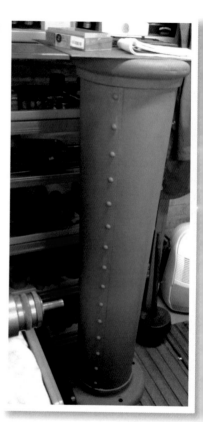

ABOVE Some of the parts including the chimney that required fabricating from original drawings.

ABOVE With the offside wheel removed, the gearing connecting the crankshaft

**LEFT &
BELOW**
No.12335 *Hilda*
attends her
first event, the
2009 Bill Targett
Memorial Rally.

ABOVE *Hilda* largely complete will soon be another engine attending rallies.

To download our latest catalogue and to view
the full range of books and DVDs visit:

www.G2ent.co.uk

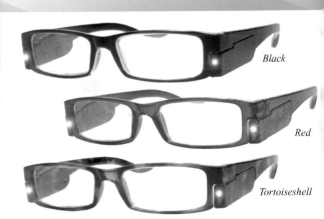

Design and artwork by David Wildish and Scott Giarnese

Published by G2 Entertainment Limited

Publishers Jules Gammond and Edward Adams

Written by Steve Lanham